P9-BZQ-571

# SHARKS SET II

# MAKO SHARKS

Adam G. Klein
ABDO Publishing Company

# visit us at
# www.abdopub.com

Published by ABDO Publishing Company, 4940 Viking Drive, Edina, Minnesota 55435.
Copyright © 2006 by Abdo Consulting Group, Inc. International copyrights reserved in all
countries. No part of this book may be reproduced in any form without written permission from
the publisher. The Checkerboard Library™ is a trademark and logo of ABDO Publishing
Company.

Printed in the United States.

Cover Photo: Visuals Unlimited
Interior Photos: Animals Animals pp. 13, 21; © C & M Fallows / SeaPics.com p. 11; © Doug
    Perrine / SeaPics.com p. 10; © James D. Watt / SeaPics.com p. 17; © Jeremy Stafford-
    Deitsch / SeaPics.com p. 5; © Richard Herrmann / SeaPics.com pp. 9, 15, 19, 23; Uko
    Gorter pp. 6-7

Series Coordinator: Heidi M. Dahmes
Editors: Heidi M. Dahmes, Megan Murphy
Art Direction: Neil Klinepier

## Library of Congress Cataloging-in-Publication Data

Klein, Adam G., 1976-
    Mako sharks / Adam G. Klein.
        p. cm. -- (Sharks. Set II)
    ISBN 1-59679-288-4
    1. Mako sharks--Juvenile literature. I. Title.

QL638.95.L3K59 2006
597.3'3--dc22

                                                                    2005041092

# CONTENTS

# Mako Sharks and Family

Mako sharks are fast, focused, and hungry. They are one of the most effective **predators** in the ocean. Mako sharks are sleek and powerful animals. Their bodies are made for speed and endurance.

There are more than 200 species of sharks. All sharks share common features. They are made of **cartilage** rather than bone. And, they are meat eaters.

There are two species of mako sharks. The shortfin mako is most common. Little is known about the longfin mako. But, many similarities exist between the two species.

Mako sharks are some of the fastest fish in the ocean. They cruise through the water at about 22 to 25 miles per hour (35 to 40 km/h). When necessary, a mako can burst up to much greater speeds.

*Unlike many sharks, makos begin hunting right after birth.*

# WHAT THEY LOOK LIKE

    Mako sharks have slender blue-gray bodies that appear deep blue in the water.  But, their bellies are white.  Mako sharks have long, pointed snouts.  And, their tails are crescent shaped to assist in swimming.

DORSAL FIN

SNOUT

EYE

MOUTH

GILL SLITS

PECTORAL FIN

The shortfin mako has large, round, black eyes.  The eyes of a longfin mako are even larger.  This feature is common in deepwater fish.  Longfin makos also have larger **pectoral** fins.

An average shortfin mako shark is between 72 and 96 inches (183 and 244 cm) long.  Larger ones weigh more than 1,000 pounds (450 kg) and are longer than 12 feet (4 m).  The longfin mako may be slightly larger.  And, female makos reach greater lengths than males.

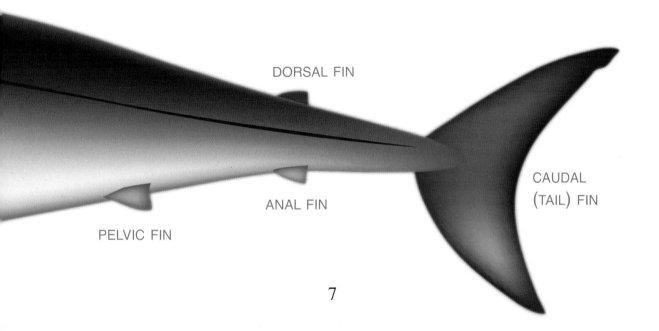

DORSAL FIN

CAUDAL (TAIL) FIN

ANAL FIN

PELVIC FIN

# WHERE THEY LIVE

Mako sharks can be found worldwide. Usually they stay in **temperate** and tropical waters. They prefer water that is between 63 and 68 degrees Fahrenheit (17 and 20°C).

Makos are active sharks. They **migrate** seasonally to warmer waters. Besides changes in water temperatures, sharks migrate because of food availability. And, some sharks migrate when they are ready to reproduce.

The distance a shark travels depends on its species. Some sharks simply move to different water depths. Others may travel 100 to 1,000 miles (160 to 1,600 km).

Mako sharks are fantastic swimmers. They can dive up to 500 feet (150 m) deep. But, they spend most of their time close to the water's surface. Makos are also able to leap out of the water. They can rush toward the surface and jump more than 20 feet (6 m) into the air!

*Mako sharks are often seen with their large dorsal fin sticking out of the water.*

# FOOD

Mako sharks use all of their abilities to hunt. Their senses help them find food from far away. Their speed allows them to swim in quickly for the kill. And, their long, bladelike

**Shortfin mako shark teeth**

teeth help makos swiftly kill their prey.

Shortfin makos eat many types of fish. They feast on tuna, swordfish, mackerel, sturgeon, and squid. They will eat other sharks, too. Makos generally leave sea mammals alone. But, sometimes they eat dolphins and sea turtles. Not much is safe from a hungry mako.

Mako sharks have a special hunting method. They chase down their prey and bite it hard. Then, they swallow their victim whole. If this does not work, the mako bites off the prey's tail. This makes the creature easier to catch because it cannot swim.

Mako sharks have bowl-shaped mouths filled with razor-sharp teeth. The teeth on the lower jaw can be seen even when the mouth is shut.

# SENSES

Mako sharks have well-developed senses for hunting. They have good vision, and they sense vibrations made by other creatures. Makos also have an incredibly sensitive sense of smell.

Like other fish, mako sharks have a lateral line system. Tiny tunnel-like canals run under a shark's skin. These canals are on both sides of its body. The lateral line senses movements and pressure changes in the water. So, a mako is always aware of its surroundings.

Sharks also possess the ability to detect electrical currents. Around a shark's head and front end are **pores** called ampullae of Lorenzini. These pores detect small electrical charges in the water.

Living creatures give off small electrical charges. A shark can locate the source of those charges with its ampullae of Lorenzini. This will lead a mako to its next meal.

Mako sharks can detect the body fluids of injured or distressed animals in the water.

# BABIES

A mako shark normally travels alone.  But, eventually it needs to mate.  A mako shark is ready to reproduce by about four to six years of age.  After mating, the female shark becomes **pregnant**.

Makos are **ovoviviparous** and carry their eggs inside of them.  That way, the babies have a better chance of surviving once they are born.  Baby mako sharks are called pups.

In the early stages, the pups live off nutrition inside their eggs.  Eventually this nutrition runs out, and they hatch from their cases.  But, the pups remain inside their mother's body.  In order to survive, the baby sharks eat other unfertilized eggs.

The shortfin mako gives birth to a **litter** of 4 to 16 sharks.  The longfin may have two pups.  Shortfins are about 26 inches (66 cm) long at birth.  Longfin pups are about 38 inches (97 cm) long.

Most sharks grow slowly. But, makos have a fast growth rate. Mako pups are born well nourished and quickly swim away from the mother.

*Shortfin makos live for about 20 years, if they are not caught by a sportfisher first.*

# ATTACK AND DEFENSE

Mako sharks are deadly hunters. They have few natural **predators**. But, makos must watch out for swordfish. This powerful fish uses its bill as a weapon. A swordfish can easily injure a mako shark.

Makos also fear humans. Adult makos are considered a prized game fish. Many people like the challenge of fishing for mako sharks. The mako's fighting ability is its best defense against humans.

Catching a mako can be very **dangerous**. They do not like to be attacked. Angry makos have destroyed boats and maimed fishers.

Mako sharks are more than game fish. They are fished for their oil, fins, skin, jaws, and teeth. The fins are used in shark fin soup. A mako shark's skin is used for leather. And, its jaws and teeth become souvenirs.

**Fishing threatens the mako shark population.**

# ATTACKS ON HUMANS

Sometimes mako sharks can be found near the shore. But, more commonly they live farther out to sea. So, they do not often come in contact with people. Still, that does not mean they are never **dangerous** to humans.

Shortfin makos are second to the white shark in reported attacks on boats. Mako sharks are known to attack boats and people if hooked by fishers. Longfin makos are not considered dangerous, but they are a threat.

Human deaths from mako attacks are rare. Sharks do not naturally prey on humans. But, humans need to respect sharks and stay clear of shark-**infested** waters.

**Only a trained professional should get this close to a mako shark.**

# MAKO SHARK FACTS

**Scientific Name:**

| | |
|---|---|
| Shortfin mako shark | *Isurus oxyrinchus* |
| Longfin mako shark | *I. glaucus* |

**Average Size:**

Mako sharks are usually 72 to 96 inches (183 to 244 cm) long.

**Where They're Found:**

Mako sharks are found in temperate and tropical waters throughout the world.

The largest mako hooked weighed 1,115 pounds (506 kg)!

# GLOSSARY

**cartilage** (KAHR-tuh-lihj) - the soft, elastic connective tissue in the skeleton.  A person's nose and ears are made of cartilage.

**dangerous** - able or likely to cause injury or harm.

**infest** - to spread or exist in large numbers so as to cause trouble or harm.

**litter** - all of the pups born at one time to a mother shark.

**migrate** - to move from one place to another, often to find food.

**ovoviviparous** (OH-voh-veye-VIH-puh-ruhs) - a fish or reptile that carries its eggs inside it while they develop.

**pectoral** - located in or on the chest.

**pore** - a small opening in an animal or plant through which matter passes.

**predator** - an animal that kills and eats other animals.

**pregnant** - having one or more babies growing within the body.

**temperate** - having neither very hot nor very cold weather.

# WEB SITES

To learn more about mako sharks, visit ABDO Publishing Company on the World Wide Web at **www.abdopub.com**. Web sites about mako sharks are featured on our Book Links page. These links are routinely monitored and updated to provide the most current information available.

# INDEX